KENT

...gland

Introduction

The beautiful county of Kent has long been known as the 'Garden of England'. The name refers, of course, to the prolific cultivation of fruit, hops and market produce which fills the area, but it also evokes the rural charm of large parts of this delightful county at the south-east corner of England. The peaceful pastoral scene is rivalled only by the individual character of each of the many seaside resorts set along the county's 126-mile-long coastline.

Kent's position, just twenty-one miles from France, has had a major effect on its growth and development. Europe's cultural influences have usually arrived first in Kent, *en route* for the capital, and consequently the county has always been in the vanguard of new developments. Conversely, advances in London have quickly reached Kent on their way to Europe.

This concept of Kent as an important thoroughfare is reinforced by the existence of the many ancient roads and trackways which traverse it, and by evidence that has been found of early settlements. Memorials dating back to around 2000 BC can be seen at Kit's Coty near Rochester. The Coldrum Stones stand near Trottiscliffe and Sarsen stones and monoliths can be found in Addington Park.

The county's main east-to-west track, the Pilgrims' Way, runs along under the escarpment of the North Downs, the ridge of hills which enter Kent north of Westerham and stretch down to the coast, reaching a dramatic climax as the White Cliffs of Dover. Most of the pilgrims heading towards Canterbury throughout the course of history would have known their route by its Roman name of Watling Street; the name Pilgrims' Way was only adopted just over a hundred years ago. The inland towns of Canterbury and Rochester are both situated on this direct route to London, and many other straight Roman roads still exist in the county.

Agriculture has always been the backbone of Kent's economy, but this area also had the first heavy industry in the country, in the form of iron-smelting, and some of the churchyards contain the iron tombstones of the early iron-masters. The cloth trade also flourished from the sixteenth century. It was not until the nineteenth century that recreation started to rival agriculture as a major employer, when the coastal resorts of Margate, Ramsgate and Broadstairs began to attract huge numbers of visitors wishing to enjoy the mild climate and fresh sea air. Today the residents of Kent have as much affection for their native county as do the millions of holidaymakers who flock there every year. Whether they were born 'men of Kent' or 'Kentish men' – that is 'east' or 'west' of the River Medway – they are all justly proud of their beautiful and diverse county.

Below: *Horsmondon Church and the Weald of Kent*

Below: *launching a fishing boat at Dungeness*
Inset: *Margate*

Coastal Kent

Along the Kent coast are some of England's most popular holiday resorts, ranging from lively seaside towns, busy with family entertainment, to more tranquil spots where time seems to have stood still.

By travelling from Sheerness in the north and following the coastline round to Dungeness in the south, the diverse spectrum of the major seaside towns can be appreciated. The sea, of course, has played a major role in the development of all of them, both through the employment it offers, and from the accessibility it affords to other regions, in England and abroad.

The Isle of Sheppey is a unique area, an internationally important wetland and an ornithologist's paradise. It is joined to the mainland by the Kingsferry Bridge, which is periodically raised to allow boats on the River Swale beneath to pass on their way. Sheerness is a former naval base, and today it still has bustling docks which handle cattle, cars, food and drink, as well as passengers wishing to cross to the Dutch port of Flushing. Both Sheerness and Leysdown have shingle beaches and numerous amusements, the former boasting a new promenade with gardens, play and picnic areas, a modern indoor swimming-pool and a leisure centre. The Leysdown Coastal Park has many safe beaches as well as an interesting nature trail, and just to the south, near Shellness, there is even a naturist beach, where nude sunbathing is acceptable.

Back on the mainland, Whitstable is a picturesque fishing port which has long been known as the 'Oyster Town'. The oyster industry has existed there for more than 2,000 years, and there is still an annual summer Oyster Festival.

6 The narrow streets provide a contrast to the beautiful open coastline of Whitstable and of Tankerton, a delightful extension of the town.

Herne Bay is a more traditional seaside town, laid out in a symmetrical fashion, with the principal roads running parallel to the sea. The seafront is about seven miles long and is backed by wooded rolling hills. From the Promenade there are marvellous views of the Thames Estuary, and of the twin towers of Reculver, which are the only remains of a Roman fortress.

Further along the coast, Margate has been a popular holiday resort since 1736, when people began to flock to the town from London. Today the resort includes the quieter beaches of Birchington, Westgate and Westbrook to the west, and Cliftonville to the east, with its cliffside walks and beautiful parks. Margate itself is a place of opposites, the old town, with its sixteenth-century Tudor House and other ancient buildings, providing a marked contrast to the thrills and spills of the gravity-defying rides at the local amusement park, and the popular entertainment provided at the Winter Gardens.

Further east again, Broadstairs still offers the old-world atmosphere which made it a favourite holiday resort for Charles Dickens. Seven bays with pleasant beaches are sheltered by cliffs and each has a charm of its own, some even affording views of France on a clear day. The steep Harbour Street has a flint arch over it called York Gate, which was built in about 1540.

Above: *Broadstairs*
Far left: *Reculver Towers*
Left: *Herne Bay*

The town of Ramsgate is built on and between two lofty chalk cliffs. Its centre is the Royal Harbour which dates back to 1749. The harbour was a front-line naval base in the Second World War and played an important part in the evacuation of allied troops from Dunkirk. It now boasts a 500-berth yacht marina. The Roman Catholic church of St Augustine, financed and built by A.W. Pugin in 1847-51, is well worth a visit, and Pugin's house, the Grange, is just next door.

A short distance from Ramsgate, the smuggling village of Pegwell sits on the clifftop overlooking Pegwell Bay Nature Reserve. Nearby, the replica Viking ship *Hugin* serves as a reminder of the original invasion of Britain by Hengist and Horsa in AD 449.

Sandwich nestles at the southern end of Pegwell Bay and is still one of the Cinque Ports, together with Hastings, Dover, Romney and Hythe, even though the main town is now about two miles inland. It was developed as a port by the Saxons, but the sea has receded since about 1500. A Flemish and Dutch atmosphere pervades the town, and the huge churches bear witness to its former importance. The ancient Barbican, a Tudor building with a chessboard pattern at its base, is particularly interesting. Sandwich is perhaps best known today for its famous golf courses.

The sister towns of Deal and Walmer, which were amalgamated in 1935, owe their existence mainly to the treacherous Goodwin Sands three miles off the coast, for in bygone days sailing ships were forced to wait in the Downs, a quiet stretch of water between the sands and the shore, for a favourable wind and tide. Standing back from the sea-front at Deal is the Timeball Tower, which was built in 1821 as a semaphore signalling tower, but which now houses a fascinating time, telegraphy and maritime communications museum. Smuggling was once rife along this stretch of the coast, and Deal's narrow streets and alleys have been the haunts of smugglers and sailors. Historical evidence suggests that Deal beach was actually the landing-point for Caesar and his legions when they invaded Britain. In August 1946, a tablet was placed near Deal Castle to mark the two thousandth anniversary of the landing. Today there are many delightful parks and gardens, including Connaught Park, on the castle hill slopes, and the gardens of Kearnsey Abbey and Bushy Ruff.

The White Cliffs of Dover are undoubtedly one of Britain's most famous landmarks, and Dover itself is a vital seaport and commercial centre. Despite its important position in the modern world, Dover still has many historic buildings which are well worth visiting. These include the Maison Dieu, a hospice for pilgrims travelling to

Top: *Ramsgate Marina and Harbour*
Left: *Dover*
Above: *the River Stour at Sandwich*

Canterbury, built in 1203 and restored in 1603. The fascinating Roman Painted House, which has been called Britain's buried Pompeii, can be found in the very heart of the town. The house features the oldest and best-preserved original wall paintings in Europe.

The North Downs reach the sea at Folkestone, a bustling seaside town which began to develop as a resort at the beginning of the eighteenth century. It retains an air of prosperity and graciousness, and the mile-and-a-half-long promenade, known as The Leas, is a marvellous place on which to sit and watch the world go by. Many entertainment venues are located along its length.

Hythe's history spans almost 2,000 years, and many unspoilt ancient buildings still remain, together with more than one hundred specialist shops in the High Street. The twenty-three-mile-long Royal Military Canal, which runs through the town, was built in 1804 as a defence against invasion by Napoleon. Originally water covered what is now Hythe's sea-front, but in 1230 it was already silting up, and by 1450 the harbour was lost. Nevertheless, Hythe prospered as a market-town. St Leonard's Church, perched on the hill, is one of the finest churches in Kent, with an exceedingly high nave, dating back to 1225. An ambulatory within it contains thousands of medieval skulls and bones which were stacked there sometime before 1500. In the churchyard lies Lionel Larkin, the inventor of the lifeboat.

Dymchurch was once a fishing village and capital of Romney Marsh, the unique, flat, open area which is dotted with numerous small churches. The three-mile-long Dymchurch Wall now provides the principal barrier against the sea. Further south, New Romney is today over a mile inland, having lost its maritime importance when a fierce storm destroyed the harbour in 1287 and permanently diverted the course of the River Rother. For centuries, ships used to anchor beneath the glorious Norman church of St Nicholas, which was sometimes flooded by the water.

Further along the coast, and forming the last Kentish coastal area before the county border with East Sussex, is Dungeness. The region is renowned for sea-fishing, and a shingle area is also the site of an extensive bird sanctuary and observatory. This unique triangle of land juts out into the Channel and is growing at a rapid rate because of the action of two opposing sea currents. A unique flora and fauna coexists there with the CEGB's fifth nuclear power station, which was completed in 1965.

This brief look at Kent's diverse coastline gives a taste of the area, but there are, of course, many smaller resorts which are also well worth a visit.

Above: *Hythe viewed from Folkestone*
Far left: *Dungeness lighthouse and nuclear power station*
Left: *St Clement's Church, Old Romney*

Literary Kent

Famous authors throughout history have lived and worked in Kent, drawing inspiration for their characters and settings from the towns and countryside around them.

Perhaps the most famous of all is Charles Dickens, whose books are full of scenes and people drawn from the places where he stayed. He spent his early childhood in Ordnance Terrace and St Mary's Place, Chatham, enjoyed many holidays in Broadstairs, and spent the last twelve years of his life at Gads Hill, near Rochester. The Swiss-style chalet where he wrote his last books now stands in the grounds of the Dickens Centre in Rochester. It features as Westgate House in *Pickwick Papers* and as the Nuns' House in *Edwin Drood*. By coincidence, William Shakespeare had also used Gads Hill for the setting of a robbery in *Henry IV.*

Dickens once said, 'I have many happy recollections of Kent and am scarcely less interested in it than if I had been a Kentish man bred and born, and had resided in the county all my life.' This affection is clearly reflected in his writing. The Royal Victoria and Bull Hotel, Rochester, appears in *Pickwick Papers* and in *Great Expectations,* the hero of which took his apprenticeship at Rochester's Guildhall. *The Mystery of Edwin Drood* is almost completely set in Rochester, renamed Cloisterham in that particular book, and known as Great Wingle-bury in *Sketches by Boz.*

Broadstairs, too, retains many Dickensian connections. *David Copperfield* was written in a house called Bleak House, where Dickens spent many holidays between 1837 and 1851, although it is not the Bleak House featured in the novel of the same name. *Nicholas Nickleby* was also finished in the town, and today there is an annual Dickens Festival held in October.

Dickens' honeymoon was spent in Chalk, near Gravesend, where he also wrote part of *Pickwick Papers.* Later in life, while living at Gads Hill, he frequented a pub in Cobham called the Leather Bottle, which is still full of Dickensian memorabilia.

One of the first writers to feature Kent in their work was Geoffrey Chaucer, whose *Canterbury Tales* have rightfully taken their place at the forefront of English literature. St George's Street in Canterbury was the birthplace of another great English writer, Christopher Marlowe. T.S. Eliot's play, *Murder in the Cathedral,* was first staged in the Chapter House of Canterbury Cathedral, near the spot where the murder of Thomas à Becket took place.

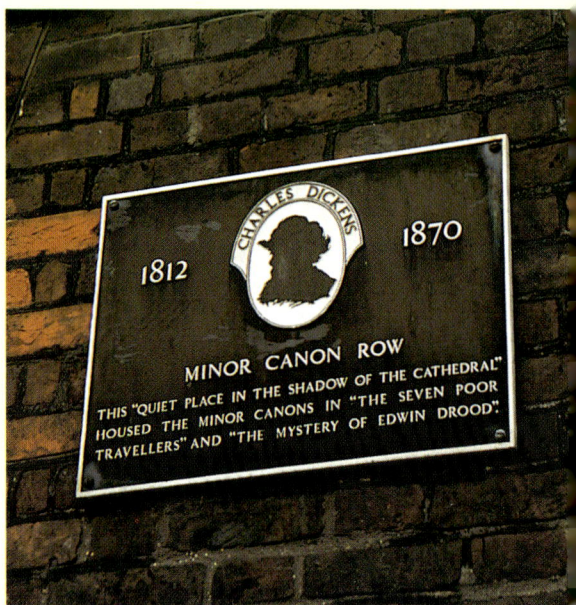

CHARLES DICKENS
1812   1870

MINOR CANON ROW

THIS "QUIET PLACE IN THE SHADOW OF THE CATHEDRAL" HOUSED THE MINOR CANONS IN "THE SEVEN POOR TRAVELLERS" AND "THE MYSTERY OF EDWIN DROOD".

Sir Philip Sidney was born at Penshurst in 1559 and featured the grounds in his *Arcadia,* while Sir Thomas Wyatt, who introduced the sonnet to England in his poems to Anne Boleyn, lived at Allington. John Donne, the great English poet, was the rector of Sevenoaks from 1616 to 1631.

The list continues, like a literary *Who's Who.* Jane Austen's brother, Edward Knight, owned Godmersham Park, so she was a frequent visitor to the area. Joseph Conrad lived for a time at 'Oswalds', Bishopsbourne, and later at Pent Farm, Postling, two miles from Hythe. One of his greatest novels, *Heart of Darkness,* is a tale told on the deck of a yacht anchored off Gravesend. H.G. Wells was born at Bromley and lived at Sandgate from 1899, while both Thackeray and E.M. Forster lived for a time at Royal Tunbridge Wells. Ian Fleming, author of the James Bond stories, bought the Old Palace at Bekesbourne and set his novel *Moonraker* in Kent.

Writers of children's books also seem to have found Kent inspiring: Edith Nesbitt, author of the *Railway Children,* lived at Romney Marsh, Halstead and Eltham; Frances Hodgson Burnett, creator of *Little Lord Fauntleroy,* lived at Great Maytham Hall, Rolvenden; Frank Richard, author of *Billy Bunter,* came from Broadstairs, and Enid Blyton from Beckenham.

Poets too have found inspiration from their Kentish surroundings. Edmund Blunden's father was headmaster at Yalding School and Blunden was much influenced by his environment. Dante Gabriel Rossetti lived and died in Birchington and is buried in the town.

Considering these extensive literary connections, it seems entirely appropriate that William Caxton, the printer who produced England's first book, was also born in the Weald of Kent. He would, no doubt, have been proud of all the famous Kentish writers who have since used his medium to entertain us.

Left: *Dickens' Swiss chalet in the grounds of the Charles Dickens Centre, Rochester*
Below left: The Mystery of Edwin Drood *is almost entirely set in Rochester*
Above: *a dramatic audio-visual display at the Charles Dickens Centre*
Below: *Penshurst Place*

Town and Country

Kent's inland towns and villages are as varied as their coastal counterparts, and archaeological remains suggest extremely early settlement in this part of Britain. Dartford, or Darentford as it was known, is among the oldest settlements in the county. Nearby, the oldest human fossil in Northern Europe, the famous Swanscombe Skull, was discovered. The skull is that of a woman who lived 250,000 years ago.

Today Dartford is a busy commercial centre which has managed to retain some character, while taking full advantage of its position just seventeen miles from central London. The town developed at the point where the Roman road of Watling Street crosses the River Darent, about a mile from where this river joins the Thames. There are several old churches, including St Margaret's at Darenth, which dates back to the tenth century and is one of the oldest churches in Britain.

Just south of Dartford is Swanley, now very much a commuter town, and to the east is the borough of Gravesham, comprising Gravesend and Northfleet, as well as the villages of Cobham, Higham, Luddesdown, Meopham and Shorne. There have been inhabitants in this area since the Stone Age. Gravesend developed because of its commanding position on the south bank of the Thames; the cross-river ferry to Tilbury is a long-established route into Essex. The town received its first charter in 1268, and a market has been held there ever since.

Above: *Aylesford Bridge and the River Medway*
Inset: *Cobham Hall*

16   Northfleet's claim to fame is as the site of the country's first cement factory, set up in an area with a long-established local chalk-cutting industry.

The City of Rochester-upon-Medway comprises the towns of Chatham, Strood and Rochester, and settlement there dates back to Roman times. In fact, the medieval city walls which can be seen in Rochester High Street follow the line of Roman fortifications. Apart from the castle, cathedral and its previously mentioned Dickensian associations, Rochester has much more to recommend it. The High Street has been restored to Victorian splendour, and the Guildhall, one of the finest seventeenth-century buildings in Kent, which was originally a centre of local government, now houses a fascinating museum. Watts Charity is probably the oldest house in Rochester and was among the bequests made by Mr Richard Watts, MP for Rochester in the reign of Elizabeth I. Until 1940 it provided six poor travellers with bed, board and fourpence each per night.

Nearby Chatham is a popular shopping centre and has proud maritime associations, like Strood, on the north bank of the Medway. St Nicholas' Church in Strood High Street was rebuilt in 1814 as the first commission of Robert Smith, who was later to design the British Museum in London. Temple Manor is another interesting building, originally built in 1240 by the Knights Templars, an order of celibate soldiers founded to protect the Holy Land.

Gillingham is now a modern centre for commerce, shopping and recreation, but many famous people are connected with its seafaring past. Lord Nelson joined his first ship here and Sir Francis Drake began his sailing career on the River Medway. One of Gillingham's most famous sons was William Adams, who established the first English trading links with Japan in the sixteenth century and has since become something of a folk hero to Japanese people.

Sittingbourne is an old market-town which was once an important stage for pilgrims on their way to Canterbury. Much later it became associated with the paper, brick, cement and boatbuilding industries. Ancient Milton Regis, which boasts the third oldest bowling-green in the country, is now inextricably merged with Sittingbourne.

Further east, Faversham has many historic buildings which make it quintessentially Kentish, and it is also surrounded by the pretty orchards and villages for which the county is renowned. The Guildhall and Market Place are particularly picturesque, and the remains of a Benedictine Abbey which was founded here in 1147 are also well worth searching out.

Clockwise from top left: *the Royal Victoria
and Bull Hotel, Rochester High Street;
Rochester's Guildhall clock; the Dolphin
Yard Sailing Barge Museum, Sittingbourne;
Chatham Historic Dockyard*

Left: *the pump in Faversham's town centre*
Below: *Christ Church Gate and Memorial, Canterbury*
Bottom: *a view of Canterbury*
Bottom right: *Canterbury Cathedral*

Canterbury is undoubtedly most famous for its cathedral, but there is much else of interest within its medieval walls. The city straddles the River Stour, and many Roman remains have been found, including those of a theatre, public baths and barrack facilities. A tessellated Roman pavement has been preserved and is on display to visitors. It is as a cradle of Christianity that that city is best known, however, and Roman silver featuring a Christian monogram was discovered in 1962, indicating just how long these religious associations have existed. The number of pilgrims visiting Canterbury reached a peak between the twelfth and sixteenth centuries, following the murder there in 1170 of Archbishop Thomas à Becket, and his canonisation in 1172. Despite the desecration of the cathedral and breaching of the city walls by Cromwell's soldiers, and the destruction caused in 1942 by wartime bombing, Canterbury still retains its essential character and charm.

South-west of Canterbury, the nearest large town is Ashford, situated in the heart of Kent and, as such, a focal point for the surrounding agricultural concerns of the area. Ashford has always been a flourishing market centre, but it is the neighbouring villages which retain most character. The lovely old village of Biddenden has a charming main street lined with timber- and brick-built houses, and with pavements made of Bethersden marble. A pair of famous Siamese twins, Eliza and Mary Chalkhurst, lived in the village in about 1100 and are commemorated on the village sign. They were joined at the hips and the shoulders and lived for thirty-four years.

Tenterden is known as the 'Jewel of the Kentish Weald'. It is indeed a charming and unspoilt market-town with a picturesque tree-lined High Street which has an air of gentility about it. The town prospered through the medieval wool trade, and became a centre for the rich weavers and ironmongers of the Weald. Two miles away is Smallhythe Place, where Dame Ellen Terry lived. Today her home is a museum devoted to the theatre. Appledore, perched on the edge of Romney Marsh, is another medieval weavers' village, and is, in some ways, a smaller version of Tenterden.

Maidstone is the county town of Kent, ideally situated midway between London and the coast, as well as being in the centre of some of England's most fertile countryside, at the foot of the Downs. The surrounding hop gardens provide hops for several large breweries, whilst the area's orchards and farms produce most of London's fruit and vegetables. The town centre has many fine buildings, including the Archbishop's Palace, once a manor owned by the Archbishop of Canterbury, and the Archbishop's Stables which now house the Tyrwhitt-Drake Museum of Carriages. Mote Park and Brenchley Gardens are two of the town's most pleasant open spaces.

West Malling and East Malling are both impressive towns to the west of Maidstone. West Malling has a beautiful wide High Street lined with many distinctive Georgian houses, rivalled only in splendour by East Malling's attractive village green. St Mary's Abbey in West Malling incorporates parts of a Benedictine nunnery founded in 1090.

It is said that it was at Aylesford, another delightful nearby village, that Hengist and Horsa defeated the Britons in the fifth century, thus allowing the English nation to come into being. In the thirteenth century the Carmelites built their first friary in England at Aylesford, a friary which is now open both to the general public and to pilgrims alike.

Tonbridge developed initially because of its strategic position on the Medway, and grew even more rapidly after 1741, when the river became a navigable waterway. The arrival of the railways in 1842 increased its importance still further, and today Tonbridge is a prosperous and thriving town. The oldest landmark is the mound on which the Saxons built a stronghold, and there are also remains of the later Norman castle which was built there.

The enchanting spa-town of Royal Tunbridge Wells acquired its prefix in 1909, and, in fact, its early growth was due to the town's popularity as a watering-place with Stuart and Hanoverian royalty. The iron-impregnated waters are still renowned for their medicinal qualities. The Pantiles, a terraced walk with shops behind a colonnade, takes its name from the original square earthenware paving tiles which were paid for by Queen Anne. They were replaced by flagstones in the eighteenth century, but the Pantiles remains a delightful place for a promenade, recreating a genteel world long since past. Today the town is an excellent shopping centre with many antique shops and bookshops, and quaint tea-rooms, as well as modern department stores.

Sevenoaks and Westerham are both sizeable towns in the west of Kent. Sevenoaks reaped the benefit of being *en route* to Tunbridge Wells when the spa there became popular, and later, when the railways arrived in 1868, from its proximity to London. Sevenoaks Grammar School was founded in 1418 by William Sennocke, a friend of Dick Whittington's, and is one of the oldest schools in the country. Westerham's main street and village green are flanked by eighteenth- and nineteenth-century houses, one of which was the home of William Pitt. Two other heroes of Westerham, General Wolfe and Sir Winston Churchill, are commemorated by statues on the green.

Left: *Westgate Gardens, Canterbury*
Above: *statue of General Wolfe, Westerham*
Top right: *The Pantiles, Royal Tunbridge Wells*
Right: *The Archbishop's Palace, Maidstone*

The Garden of England

Kent is indeed the 'Garden of England', renowned for its hops, orchards, vegetables and sheep above all else, but also gaining recognition for its grapes, nuts and other produce.

Hop gardens are a familiar sight throughout the county, the sweet-smelling hops having been introduced into England from Flanders as a commercial crop in 1524. Kent, Surrey and Essex were the first counties in which they were grown, and today the fields around Faversham, Canterbury, the Medway, Yalding and Goudhurst are among the major hopgrowing areas in the country, the hops flourishing particularly well in the alluvial loam soils of the sheltered valleys.

The hops are used for flavouring and preserving beer, even though, in Henry VIII's time, it was an offence to use them for making beer more bitter, for fear that they caused 'lunacy and physical deformity'. The familiar oast-houses are used for drying the hops. Early oast-houses were simple, barn-like buildings, but in the eighteenth century they were built as square kilns topped with a wooden cowl. By the nine-teenth century, the circular kiln had been adopted and it is this type which is widely seen today.

Faversham has been a centre for brewing since local monks began producing ale about 800 years ago. Today, two breweries still thrive there – Kent's only independent brewer, family-owned Shepherd Neame, and one of Whitbread's most successful breweries, Fremlins. Whitbread Hop Farm at Beltring features unique Victorian oast-houses and is a good place at which to learn more about the history of hopgrowing in Kent. Shepherd Neame has been in Faversham for almost 300 years and now brews around 156,000 barrels, or 45 million pints (26 million litres), of beer each year. Kentish hops, such as Wye Challenger and Northdown, are used to impart the distinctive bitter flavour, and local barley and water is also used. Guided tours of the brewery are available.

Today Shepherd Neame has diversified into producing wine from Müller Thurgau grapes grown in a six-acre vineyard at Queen's Court

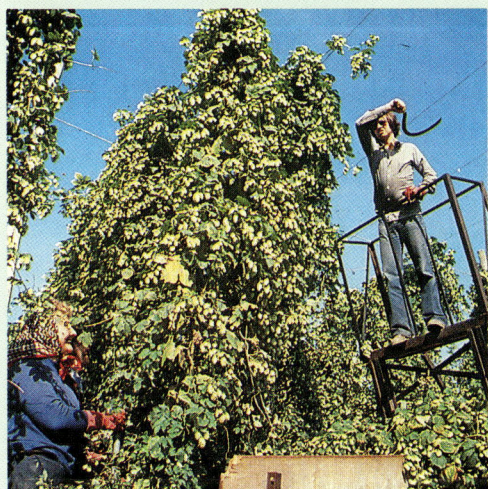

Opposite: *orchards near Sissinghurst*
Above: *hopfields and oasthouses*
Left: *harvesting hops*
Below: *hopfield near Goudhurst*

Farm, Ospringe, and there are numerous other independent vineyards scattered throughout the county. Biddenden Vineyards near Ashford, Penshurst Vineyards, Syndale Valley Vineyards at Newnham, Tenterden Vineyards, Lamberhurst Priory Vineyards and St Nicholas of Ash Vineyards all take advantage of the county's sunny climate and fertile soils to produce tasty wines from local grapes.

The county is equally famous for its fruit-growing, the establishment of which is also attributed to Flemings who arrived in the middle of the sixteenth century. It is known that in 1553 a certain Richard Harrys, fruiterer to Henry VIII, imported various cherry and pear grafts to plant on land belonging to the King at Teynham, near Sittingbourne. Today one third of the farmland in the Kentish Weald is devoted to orchards of every description, which supply fruit to London and other important markets. Apples, cherries, currants, raspberries, pears and plums all grow to perfection in the mild climate and deep soil, and the sought-after Kentish Cob nut is also occasionally grown.

Traditionally many of the orchards are grazed by sheep, and the county is famous for these hardy animals, which thrive both in the heart of the blossom country and on the drained pastures of such seemingly inhospitable places as Romney Marsh. In spring the amusing antics of the young lambs under the blossom-laden branches creates a typically Kentish scene.

Many top-quality vegetables are also grown in Kent for the London markets, and there is even a herb farm at Iden Croft, near Staplehurst, which grows more than 450 varieties of herbs. What more appropriate name for Kent, then, than 'The Garden of England'?

Below: *Hever Castle*
Inset, top: *Rochester Cathedral*
Inset, bottom: *Rochester Castle*

Kent has more history contained within its boundaries than any other county. Separated from Europe by only twenty-one miles of sea, it has been sporadically invaded by foreign powers since Roman times. In AD 596 there was also a more peaceful 'invasion' of the county, when St Augustine and his monks landed at Ebbsfleet and brought Christianity to England. The ancient houses, castles, abbeys and cathedrals of Kent reflect the county's fascinating history.

Rochester Castle has one of the finest and best-preserved square keeps in the country and was originally built to defend the Medway crossing, where there had been a battle with the invading Romans in AD 43. Bishop Gundulph erected a castle here in 1080 and shortly afterwards, in 1126, William de Corbeuil, Archbishop of Canterbury, erected the huge keep, the tallest in England. Defenders held out for two months against King John, but a corner of this massive keep was eventually brought down when the King's forces undermined it and then set fire to the pit-props supporting it by using the fat of forty pigs.

Rochester Cathedral stands in the shadow of the castle, and the Bishopric of Rochester is the second oldest in the country, having been founded by St Augustine in AD 604. A Saxon cathedral on the site was destroyed and rebuilt several times before the same Bishop Gundulph who was responsible for the castle began a new cathedral, which was consecrated on Ascension Day 1130 in the presence of Henry I. Like the castle, the cathedral was sacked by King John, but massive rebuilding took place and by the fifteenth century the nave had been made much lighter by the addition of large windows and the Lady Chapel had been added. Although Rochester Cathedral is modest in size in comparison with other cathedrals, the crypt is one of the finest in the country.

Chilham Castle is not one castle, but two, the old Norman keep standing behind a Jacobean mansion which was erected in the seventeenth century. The original castle here was probably built of wood and occupied an important defensive position above the River Stour, with a view through to Canterbury, but this early structure was replaced in the twelfth century by the great octagonal keep which is now one of only two in the country. The Jacobean mansion was built in 1616 for Sir Dudley Digges, James I's Master of the Rolls. The grounds are a delight to visit, some of them refashioned by Capability Brown, and there are splendid terraced and topiary gardens as well as a heronry. Legend dictates that if the herons do not return to Chilham by St Valentine's Day each year, the owner of the estate will meet a terrible fate.

Scotney Castle near Lamberhurst similarly comprises two castles. The 'modern' castle is a Gothic building of 1837 by Anthony Salvin, standing on high ground from where paths lead down to reach a lake and the romantic ruins of a much earlier building. This is a fourteenth-century manor house which was enlarged in Tudor and Stuart times, and which stands surrounded by a moat.

Penshurst Place is the finest example of a medieval mansion in the country. Sir John de Pulteney, a merchant prince who was four times Lord Mayor of London, started the present building in 1340 and built the magnificent Great Hall with its ten life-sized figures looking down on visitors from the chestnut-beamed roof. In 1552 Edward VI presented Penshurst Place to his chamberlain, Sir William Sidney, with whose family the ownership has remained ever since. Today armour and weapons from all ages are on display in the crypt, whilst in the long gallery there is the leaden death-mask of Queen Elizabeth I.

Knole House, just south of Sevenoaks, takes its name from the knoll upon which it stands. It is immense, having seven courtyards, fifty-two staircases and 365 rooms, and it stands in a park which is six miles in circumference. Archbishop Bouchier was the first great builder at Knole: he transformed what was then a collection of unimpressive buildings into a palace, and examples of his work can still be seen in the main entrance and principal courtyard. After many other changes of ownership, Knole was given by Elizabeth I to her cousin, Thomas Sackville, in 1566, and the Sackville ownership continued until the property was handed over to the National Trust in 1946. The mansion is now a treasure-house of furniture and paintings, surrounded by a 1,000-acre deer-park.

Sissinghurst Castle is another property whose remarkable state of preservation is

Top: *Chilham Castle*
Above: *Scotney Castle*
Centre right: *Leeds Castle*
Right: *Ightham Mote, near Sevenoaks*

largely due to a member of the Sackville family.
Victoria Sackville-West, the authoress, was actually born at Knole, but fell in love with this Tudor mansion and set about restoring it with her husband after it had been neglected for many years. She died there in 1962, after creating some of the loveliest gardens in Kent, and the property passed into the hands of the National Trust in 1968.

Also owned by the National Trust is Chartwell, another delightful Tudor house which passed through many hands before Sir Winston Churchill bought the estate for £5,000 in 1921. He completely transformed the building into a modern home, remodelling and rebuilding where necessary. The gardens too received much personal attention and Churchill himself built the brick wall surrounding the kitchen garden. He was also largely responsible for what he termed his 'waterworks', a series of lakes and waterfalls which attract many waterfowl.

The picturesque moated castle of Hever was the home of Anne Boleyn and is now one of the few inhabited medieval castles in the country. It was originally built as a manor house by Thomas de Hever and subsequently replaced with a castle by Sir Geoffrey de Boleyn, Anne's great-grandfather. It was at Hever that Henry VIII first met Anne and it was here that he courted her. Her ghost is said to haunt the castle once a year on Christmas Eve. Henry later gave the castle to his divorced fourth wife, Anne of Cleves, who kept it for seventeen years. After that it changed ownership many times before being bought by the American Astor family, who completely restored it, creating the thirty-five-acre lake, together with the wonderful gardens, maze and a yew hedge cut as a set of chessmen.

Leeds Castle, named after Led, Chief Minister of Ethelbert IV, King of Kent in AD 857, stands on two islands in the centre of a moat and was aptly described as 'the loveliest castle in the world' by Lord Conway. A royal residence for over 300 years, the castle was a favourite home for eight of England's medieval queens. Now lovingly restored, it contains a magnificent collection of medieval furnishings, French and English furniture, tapestries and Impressionist paintings. There is also a unique collection of dog collars. The castle stands within 500 acres of beautiful parkland and there is even a vineyard, where the castle's own wine is produced.

Another moated castle is Allington, which began as a fortified manor house in 1282 and which was extensively altered and rebuilt by the Wyatt family in the sixteenth century. It later went through a long period of decline and came close to demolition in the nineteenth century, but in 1905 restoration was begun by Sir Martin Conway. In 1951 the castle was sold to the

Top: *Penshurst Place*
Above: *Dover Castle*
Right: *Squerryes Court, near Westerham*
Far right: *Canterbury Cathedral*

Carmelite friars who, a few years earlier, had returned to their nearby medieval priory at Aylesford, and the castle is now run as a Christian centre.

Boughton Monchelsea Place, south of Maidstone, originally dates back to Saxon times and was once owned by Thomas Wyatt of Allington Castle. It has had a varied and interesting history, and is essentially a medieval manor house with several later additions.

In direct contrast is the garrison of Dover Castle, which has stood since Norman times. Henry II completely rebuilt the first castle, raising the great keep and erecting the strong outer walls which have been severely tested throughout the castle's long history. More romantically, the castle seems to have been a favourite residence for royal newly-weds, with Edward II, Richard II, Charles I and James II all staying there with their spouses.

Also on the coast, Lympne, Deal and Walmer castles are all fine examples of fortified strongholds. Lympne looks out over Romney Marsh and the sea along to Dungeness, and it dates from 1360 although parts of it are much older. Deal Castle is the largest in the network of Tudor coastal defences on the south coast built in 1539 by order of Henry VIII; it is a powerful moated fort with 119 gun positions. Walmer has the same design, of a circular central keep with four bastions, and has been the home of both the Duke of Wellington and Mr W.H. Smith, of bookshop fame.

Fort Amherst at Chatham is the best example left in the country of a Georgian fortress, having been constructed in 1756 to protect the Royal Naval Dockyard from landward attack and modernised between 1802 and 1811. The dockyard itself, known as the cradle of Britain's sea power, closed in 1984, but is now open to visitors.

Back in the heart of Kent, Owletts near Cobham is an impressive property which was built between 1683 and 1684 for Bonham Hayes, whilst Squerryes Court in Westerham is a privately-owned red-brick William and Mary building which is often open to the public.

No survey, however brief, of Kent's historic buildings can be complete without a mention of Canterbury Cathedral, with its marvellous blending of architectural styles and fascinating history. It contains, among other delights, massive early Norman work, the more delicate late Norman choir of William of Sens, and the Gothic splendour of a nave designed by the master-mason, Henry Yevele. Crowning the building is the great Tudor tower, which was finished in 1498 by John Wastell. The stained-glass windows are another marvel, while the cathedral precincts are also full of charm.

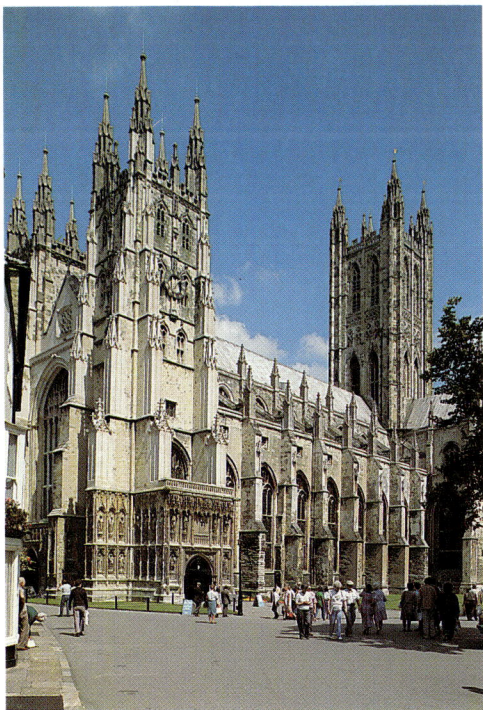

Leisure and Pleasure

Kent boasts an unrivalled selection of recreational facilities. Most of the larger towns have museums, and even some of the smaller ones have surprisingly important items on display. Dartford Borough Museum, for example, contains the Darenth Bowl, a priceless early Christian relic, which was discovered in the area in 1978, and which dates back to the fifth century. Many other museums in the county are specialist museums, such as the Battle of Britain Museum in Hawkinge, the Royal Engineers' Museum in Chatham and the Museum of Kent Rural Life in Maidstone.

For sporting enthusiasts, the list is endless. There are many excellent swimming-pools, including those at Strood Sports Centre, the Black Lion Pool at Gillingham and the Fairfield Pool at Dartford. Ice-skaters can enjoy the Ice Bowl at Gillingham, a full-size rink which was opened in 1984, and which has the added attraction of worldwide satellite television, with the county's biggest video screen. Golfers have numerous courses, including the Royal St George's at Sandwich and the Royal Cinque Ports at Deal, both of which have been the venue for international matches.

The Grand Prix racing circuit of Brands Hatch began life in the 1920s as a motorcycle grass track, but today it is famous for top-class motor-racing which also takes place at Lydden. Perhaps not quite so fast – but equally thrilling – is the horseracing which takes place at Folkestone racecourse.

For those who enjoy a slower pace of life, there are several railways from which to view the Kent countryside. The Kent and East Sussex Railway is a full-size steam railway operating from Tenterden, and running for four miles through the Rother Valley to Wittersham Road. The Sittingbourne and Kemsley Light Railway runs on a two-foot-six-inch gauge, with steam-hauled locomotives, whilst the Romney, Hythe and Dymchurch Railway starts at Hythe and ends at Dungeness, fourteen miles away, and runs a superb fleet of one-third-size passenger steam and diesel locomotives. The railway opened in 1927 and continues to delight both adults and children.

A wide variety of animals and birds are on view at the various zoos and animal parks in the county, and the largest collection of macaws and cockatoos in Europe can be seen in the

ten acres of gardens at Blean Bird Park near 31 Canterbury. John Aspinall has two collections in Kent of rare and endangered animals: at Howletts Zoo Park, Bekesbourne, near Canterbury, there is the largest breeding colony of gorillas in the world, and at Port Lympne Zoo Park there are rhinos, chimps, monkeys and many other animals. Stone Lodge Farm Park near Dartford is a traditional working farm, featuring heavy horses and rare breeds of farm animals. More heavy horses can be seen at the Dunrobin Shire Horse Stud at Greatstone, near New Romney.

The great outdoors is one of Kent's best assets, however, and full advantage can be taken of it at various country parks, such as Capstone Farm Country Park near Chatham, Queen Down Warren near Hartlip, the South Swale Nature Reserve, and many others. Bedgebury Pinetum and Forest, south of Goudhurst, has Britain's foremost collection of coniferous trees, and there are literally hundreds of beautiful gardens open to the public throughout the county.

Opposite: *The Romney, Hythe and Dymchurch Railway*
Top left: *Brands Hatch*
Left: *tiger at Port Lympne Zoo Park*
Below: *Blean Bird Park, near Canterbury*

Acknowledgement
The publishers are grateful to Rochester-upon-Medway City
Council for permission to use illustrations on pages 12 (top)
and 13 (top), and to Shepherd Neame Ltd, Faversham, for
permission to use the illustration of hop harvesting on
page 23.